AF823006

The Art of Visualization

Simply Presented

Torkom Saraydarian

T.S.G.
PUBLISHING FOUNDATION, INC.

The Art of Visualization, simply presented

ISBN: 0-929874-61-7

Library of Congress Catalog Card Number: 96-61710

Printed in the United States of America

Printed by: *KNI Incorporated*
Anaheim, California

Published by **T.S.G. Publishing Foundation, Inc.**
Complete Line of Torkom Saraydarian's Works
P.O. Box 7068, Cave Creek, AZ 85327 USA
Tel: 480-502-1909 * Fax: 480-502-0713
www.tsgfoundation.org

All visualizations are given as guidelines. They should be used with discretion and after receiving professional advice.

Table of Contents

"Dedicated in memory of my beloved brother, Yervand Galoostian."

Mariam Calonne

Preface

The Art of Visualization is a transcription of a series of classes given by Torkom Saraydarian on the expanded use of mental exercises. They are given here exactly as he conducted his classes.

At the end of each chapter is a summary of the exercise. The teacher or student can read through the text to get a full idea of how to proceed, then use the summary page to practice the visualization.

Do each exercise slowly and deliberately. Do not hurry. Follow all instructions and suggestions exactly as they are given.

It is advised that you only do one lesson per week. You can repeat any lesson for one week or more until you feel you can do it, then move on to the next one. It is also advisable that you read the entire text first before doing the visualizations. There are many explanations and directions given throughout that you will find very helpful.

As with all meditations, exercises, and visualizations, it is recommended that you always consult with a medical doctor before proceeding.

The Publisher

Introduction

These simple, introductory exercises are a good way to begin the entire series of lessons. Do these first, they will prepare you for the more complex exercises.

Sit relaxed, spine erect, close your eyes. Focus your mind. Do not let thoughts interfere.

First week. Visualize a square with black lines. For one week, every day for ten minutes, do this exercise.

Second week. Visualize that the sides of the square have colors, red, blue, green, and orange. Red on top, green on the bottom, blue on the right side, orange on the left side. The square must be seen with these colors.

Third week. Visualize that the square will turn for one minute to the right, next minute to the left, for ten minutes.

Fourth week. Visualize that the square is stable. Do not move it, but the colors will move clockwise. Where there was red, orange comes, and so on. Every time a color is shifted, you hear a note. So if the colors are moving faster you have successive notes. To keep hearing these notes is very important.

After four weeks, start from the first week and continue with the second, third, and fourth weeks. This can be done for six months to gain good control over the exercises.

Note:

1. These exercises help you focus your mind and practice concentration.

2. They teach how to control certain fluctuations and prevent the densification of thoughtforms.

3. They create color and sound and movement in our stable thoughtform.

4. They help to draw some lower energies into the higher centers and use them on mental levels.

5. They cultivate observation, attention, and control on the mental plane.

When you are finished with the square you can start practicing the same way with a triangle.

Then do the same with a cross.

These exercises are very beneficial for your health, happiness, success, and inner contacts.

The Art of Visualization

First Class

I am so happy that so many people have come to these classes. It is a marvelous indication that your soul is striving toward perfection. Really, that is so beautiful! I personally thank you for being here. Now you are going to work very hard.

The theory is this: Creative imagination, visualization, thinking create energy in your etheric system, and this energy is very real. This energy accumulates in its forms in your etheric body, then slowly penetrates into your mental plane, into your brain, into your nervous system, into your whole aura.

There is no escape when we are thinking. We are creating a motion of energy with special patterns, with special forms, with special directions, and with special frequencies.

The whole creation is based on thought — Divine Thought. Divine Thought in different esoteric traditions is called ideation, *divine ideation.* Divine ideation penetrates into spirit and matter and creates forms. These forms are all that you are seeing. This globe is a thoughtform. This solar system is a thoughtform. Divine ideation penetrated into spirit and matter and molded spirit and matter according to the thought that was projected into them.

Question: Could you explain how we create emotional energy in special forms when we think?

Answer: This energy we are creating in the mental plane slowly goes to the emotions and to the etheric body in the same patterns but in different formations. Why in different formations? It is because in our etheric body we have thousands of forms. They are active energies or forces. In the astral body we have jealousy, hatred, malice, revenge, fear, and anger. All these are in our emotional body. When that thoughtform is descending there, it is creating different patterns. But if we persist in these exercises, we are going to clean everything.

The first exercise is very simple. The first exercise is an equal-armed cross. Now if you do it right, with all your intention, with all your effort, you will benefit from it. But if you close your eyes and play with it, you will not benefit. This is why I waited so long. Later you will see what exercises are coming. They will totally transform you, but you need to do them. For example, I bring a plate of nice food. If you do not eat and digest it, it does not work.

What is this equal-armed cross? It is the symbol of balance. It is the symbol of equilibrium. It is the symbol of mental right judgment. It is the symbol of emotional equilibrium. It is the symbol of the balanced activities of our life. There are hundreds of meanings. It is so important that you realize from the beginning that you do not have a balanced life. These energies slowly will balance your judgment, your thinking, your relating.

In our relationships there is no balance. We love crazily.

We hate crazily. Our decisions are not balanced. The four-armed cross is the symbol of equilibrium. If you create this in your mental plane and it becomes a fixed image there, it will attract energy from higher realms. The Tibetan Master says energy follows thought. Create a thought and energy will come. This is a beautiful science, and you are going to learn this sooner or later because you cannot go on like this — coming Sundays and listening to some lectures and going home and forgetting about them. It must be discipleship. You are coming to college. In college you are learning your lessons and graduating.

What are we doing now? We are creating this cross in your higher mind through visualization or creative imagination or thinking. It is so simple, but you can do it five percent, you can do it fifty percent, or you can do it one hundred percent. When you are doing it one hundred percent, all your body will electrify. You will feel it. Electrification of your body is the sign that thought is creating energy. Sometimes people will cry, but you are going to do that. I am going to give you an exercise and from many facets, many viewpoints I am going to make that cross be established in your mental plane.

Question: Is the cross a symbol of a transmitter of energy?

Answer: Every symbol is a transmitter of energy. There is no symbol that cannot transmit energy. We must even call them "symbol thoughts." If you are thinking, for example, a hateful thought, energy enters into the hateful thought and creates hatred, creates emotional, physical, and mental conditions in which you are caught in hate. This is very simple, but modern psychology does not know about it at all. This is very serious, and you can benefit from it.

I am emphasizing the symbol of balance. Right thinking is balanced thinking. Right feeling is balanced feeling. If you are interested, you can see there is no balance in your life at all. Why not? It is because there is no pattern. All beautiful and ugly things in your life are based on a pattern or on chaos. If you are manifesting a virtue, you have a prototype there. If you are manifesting a vice, there is chaos there, especially in this life. Our children, our friends, we are in chaos — television chaos, movie chaos, reading chaos, chaos of politics, chaos of economics — and we lose our consciousness in confusion. What does confusion mean? It is lack of balance. We must stick to that principle of balance.

Question: When you say balance of the emotions and balance of the thoughts, what is the balance between? It cannot be good and bad. It cannot be negative and positive.

Answer: For example, you are aspiring for so much beauty, but you are not creating any beauty. You are unbalanced. You are praying, "Lord, save me and take me to heaven," but you come down and curse everybody. What kind of balance is that?

Balance is to think about beauty and to create beauty, to balance it, the subjective and objective side. You are creating here a weight, and then you are putting something weighted, balanced there. These kinds of things need hours to explain, but I am thinking that you will be able, slowly, slowly, by watching and observing your life, to find out why you are not in balance. You are in emotional imbalance, physical imbalance, activity imbalance. For example, all day you are sleeping and working only five minutes. There is no balance. Balance is not between evil and good because they cannot be balanced. If ninety percent you are good and ten percent evil, you think you balanced your life. That is not the case. Balance is not opposite poles. Please understand these things because they are very, very beautiful.

This is a very simple lesson, and I will try to take you out step by step. You will see in one week's time that you are thinking in a balanced way.

For example, you are making five hundred dollars from a man and giving that man five cents' help. You are unbalanced. Did you see that? It is so subtle, but you are going to see it clearly in your own life because you are the laboratory. You are working in your own laboratory and finding why you are not balanced.

What will happen if you are balanced? If you are balanced, first of all you will be successful. Money will pour in for you, but you are going to spend and deal with the money in a balanced way. Five thousand dollars come, and you give three thousand to somebody. Balance it. Second, it creates mental clarity, mental clarity that you can take any subject, any object, and go five hours into it. It is mental clarity because all levels in the mind are balanced. When they are balanced, *they receive balanced energies*. This is very important. When your mind is in confusion, you receive from the planet confused states of currents. You cannot receive balanced currents. When the mind is flooded with unbalanced currents, you are crazy. That is all. They will take you to the asylum.

The first lesson will go like this so that I establish the foundations.

First of all I must say that there is no danger at all. There is no danger psychiatrically, psychologically, mystically, metaphysically in what you are doing. You are just imagining. First of all that fear must be evaporated. I did these exercises for years and years. I started at age nine and continued in various shapes and depths, and I did not see any damage in it. On the contrary, these exercises cleaned the pollution that I gathered around me from certain places. This is the time that you clean your mental plane. Time is going, and you are playing with life and time and saying, "I am okay." You really are not okay. You do not know it.

Some people who are here, for example, think they are students of ours, but they did not penetrate into their skin yet. All my intention through these exercises is to help you penetrate into deeper and deeper layers. Once you find the real layer, then you will see what a glory thinking is. Read my book, *Thought, and the Glory of Thinking*. There is no book like that which has been written.

Exercise:

1. Now we are closing our eyes. We are really starting. Imagine a big flat wall, maybe twenty by twenty, forty by forty. Imagine that. Can you imagine a big wall? Now I am going to go very slowly about this so that you have time slowly, slowly to actualize that, a big wall. Let us say the color is green or white. Stand in front of that wall and see the wall in that color. Now one thing you must be very careful of, do not stress your eyes. Be very relaxed. Do not force your eyes to see. Let it come by itself. Any stress is not beneficial.
2. Look at that wall. It is blank. Touch it with your hands. Look at the texture of the wall and go from one side to the other side, touching.

3. Now sit five feet away and see that a line is coming vertically from the top to the bottom, two inches, four inches, a line. Now firm your condition again, the wall and the line. They are real, not unreal. It is very simple.
4. Now take chalk or something and trace it, a vertical line, two, three inches wide. Paint it or draw it. Make it so real that it is there, and the color, whatever color you like, put it there.
5. Visualize for a few minutes. Then open your eyes.

When you strain your eyebrows, it means there is confusion in you. You are going to relax and not strain yourself. I relaxed and here the wall came in front of me, a peach wall. Okay the line, a green line. Now I am looking at the line and observing if it is moving. Is it disappearing and coming? Is it zigzagging, or is it a firm, beautiful line? Now what is your experience?

Now you understood that when the line vacillates and undulates and goes zigzag it means something very psychological. It means your mental waves are not stabilized and are not under your control. We bring them under our control by focusing our mind in a straight line. It may take one week. It may take two weeks for you to do this. You can do this at home, and eventually the line from above becomes real. At the middle it may zigzag, belly dance, but eventually you see you can control it. How do you control it? It is by gaining control over your mind.

You understand that the mind says, "Precisely I want to see a clear line. I do not like that zigzag. Clean it!" If it is not clean, I take a chalk in my hand and draw it, clean. The first exercise, the first class will take a little time so that you know the mechanism of it, because the rest will be based on the same thing but with colors, with sounds, with fragrance, with movements. It will be fantastic, but if you did not do the first thing right, then you will say, "I cannot do it." Then you will be graduated in four weeks, but you only ate salad.

Question: When you feel energy, what is it saying to you about the quality of your visualization?

Answer: The quality of your visualization will slowly indicate that your mind is becoming balanced. You are receiving equilibrized energy. However, most of you are receiving energy from the planet from one side or from the other side, from two centers or from four centers, or even from one center. That is also disequilibrium. I am opening you slowly so that you see it. Only your mind is receiving energy. Your body is not. You are not balanced. As I told you, the foundation of success, health, happiness, longevity is balance. You are not balanced. You caused a fight, and you lost your temper. Whoever does not lose his temper wins. Do you understand that? Try it. You beat him and killed him. You are unbalanced.

Question: What is the sensation you would experience if you receive a balanced energy?

Answer: First of all, do not expect any sensation, any registration. Blindly do the exercises. Then things open. That is why, when they were taking initiations in olden mysteries in the Temples, they would bring the initiate with closed eyes, covered. It means you are a blind and ignorant man. You must not see reality immediately, but slowly your eyes will open.

It is very dangerous and very humiliating to expect immediately a reward when you do something. Here, the penny is yours. This is not business. The result may come ten years later. I did an exercise for six months, eight months, nine months, and there was no result. The Teacher said, "Do not look for results." Okay, I did the exercise and said, "There are no results." Fifty years later I was doing something and a sense opened.

Nothing is lost in your spiritual striving. Every bit of striving is accumulating in your psyche. Nothing is lost, and this will accumulate and accumulate, and suddenly when the time is ripe it will reward you.

Nature does not work as you work. "Here are ten dollars. Give me tomatoes." In these exercises, you give ten dollars and forget it. Tomatoes will come one hundred years later. That is why the Master says, "Do not work for results." But people are used to results. They work eight hours and get a salary. This is not a business. This is a faith, an intuitional recognition that whatever is planted in life will grow and bring the result, good or bad.

Question: Why is touch better than sight?

Answer: Touch is bringing you to reality. It is touch. It is emotions. It is thought. It is idea. It is visualization. All of these will be combined. If you give me time, you will see what will happen. It is a science and an art, and I was born in this science. I am not flattering myself. I need yet millions of years to go ahead, but I am born in it from monastery to monastery, from temple to temple, from Teacher to Teacher, hungry, naked. I did not know how I was living. I paid the price by riding a horse for three days without food and, reaching the Teacher, fell at his feet fainting. He asked, "Who are you?" I did not have energy to talk, but I proved that I would die to achieve my goals.

6. Close your eyes. Now see the same wall. This time the wall is on the floor. The wall is the floor and there is a big line from the top down, from north to south. Start to see the wall now. Try to see the line and step on the line and walk to the top on the straight line. Your steps will be very careful. Now come back. Go again. Come back. Now kneel beside it and feel it with your hands, the straight line. Go slowly, slowly to the top; then come back to the bottom, feeling it in your palms.
7. Now start from the beginning. When you go to the middle, see a horizontal line. Keep your eyes closed. Now it became a cross. It has no religious indication. Just sit at the middle and see from both eyes, right and left lines. They are the same color, the same thickness, the same texture. Now come to the bottom and look at the cross, big cross, forty feet by forty feet. Is it stable? Is it moving? Is it changing? You decide which color and stand on that color.
8. Go to the middle now. This is the crux of the exercise. Now in the middle you stay and suddenly see that you are four people, not one. One is going above. One is going down. One is going right. One is going left. If you can make it, I will say, "Bravo." If you cannot do, go again and again to the center and try. This may take psychosomatic sickness totally from you if you can really do it.

Now this was a little test to make you familiar with the exercises. I think that you did quite well. Now give me a report.

Question: Twice you said, "*If* you can," and twice the image faded away and I had to reconsolidate it because you said, "*If*."

Answer: You will go through hell and heaven to do these things. If you are sincere, you will do really mathematically correct and do not fluctuate by what you hear. If you cannot do it, you will try again and again. Eventually you will see how beautiful it is. When you start learning to write, you cannot. Then a day comes that you write so beautifully. If you give up and say, "I cannot do these things," then where are you progressing?

Yesterday a man was telling me that he was a seventh degree initiate. I said, "Do not make me nauseated." "What?" he said. "I am feeling nauseated," I said. What kind of stupidity is this? They are an initiate of the fifth or sixth degree. They are wise men, this or that, but in actualization they are nothing! God looks at your actualization, not at your propaganda about yourself. Eventually you will be so clear that I will say, "Close your eyes and see a dancing girl with fantastic clothing," and you will see it like a movie. In my darkest hours, the darkest tunnel, I saved myself through such a kind of visualization.

Question: Are you supposed to observe and watch yourself as four people, or are you to be those four people?

Answer: You are to be four people.

Question: When you are doing the horizontal, what if one side is harder to visualize?

Answer: If one side is harder to visualize, your left brain or right brain is not functioning in the same frequency. It is so simple. Right brain and left brain, this or that, they are not functioning. Right is functioning twenty percent, left is five percent. These balanced exercises will be done in universities, in colleges, instead of teaching trash, competition, exploitation, how to screw people and take their money. Really! It is sickening. Where are these universities? Universities should be independent, intellectual, and spiritual organizations which work only for the benefit of mankind, not for the benefit of themselves. It is working for the benefit of the people that eventually will save this planet, if it is possible. Most universities are engaged in intellectual masturbation.

Question: I am going much ahead of myself and getting impatient to get there. What does this mean?

Answer: Yes. There is automatic and mechanical following or conscious following of these things. The second is controlled start and stop so that you get control over your mind. Your mind is seeing a beautiful thing. "Stop." Stop. "Erase." Erase. Start again another phenomenon. This is what is beneficial, not your automatic, mechanical desire. Actually, the Teacher will be very clever to break any automatism that is settling in your mind because you will not benefit from it. You will be self-hypnotized. The Teacher will break it. I saw that a few people were struggling. I stopped so that they learn to start again. Imagination must not run the show, but conscious manipulation of energies must be emphasized. So, if you judge me less you will benefit more.

Question: When we separate and become four people, are we to go clear out to the ends of the arms?

Answer: Yes, both arms, here, there, there, but there is a trick in it. For example, you imagine that you are going there. You are not going to imagine. You are becoming those four persons. Now what is happening? Let me explain this one.

Most of the time because of the conditions of life, your etheric and emotional and mental bodies are "hashed." You have much difficulty to release yourself from this congestion. We call this "psychic congestion." This exercise opens it, opens it, and if you do it right you will see that you are feeling tremendously free. Some joy is coming in you because the congestion is gone. There are many, many more sublevels of this than I have said.

Question: Going back to the four people, do you see one and the other and the other and the other or do you try to see them all at one time?

Answer: It is all at one time. It is not easy but if you give up and say, "It is not easy," you did not get anything. You are going to do it. You are going to take a pencil and learn Arabic, Hebrew, Armenian, and remember it, do it. If you do not do it, you can listen and four weeks later you say, "That was good." Even if it was no good, whatever you did was a benefit. Life collects all little strivings. I want you to understand this point. It is so beneficial. It is so good to know it. Every effort you make for spiritual perfection is not lost. It accumulates and accumulates, and whenever it comes into a certain degree, it creates results.

Question: What causes this "hashing" that you are talking about?

Answer: "Hashing" is very easy to understand. Suddenly you are walking and your mommy says, "You are crazy!" You are hashed. Then a man says, "Your ideas are stupid!" You are hashing yourself, or in such kinds of circumstances you are hashed.

You must go and think about it. What I am saying is not the whole story. It is just seeds of thoughts. You are going to meditate, find out, and say, "For these four lectures I am going to be very serious."

Question: When you are divided into four or see four of you, are you also one in the middle?

Answer: It is just four.

Do not panic when you try to do these things and are not able to do them and then go home and say, "Goodness, I could not do it." It is totally normal that you cannot do it. I know that. You will not be able to do it, but you will be able to break the resistance. Once you break the resistance, things will be done for you. I am saying do not force yourself. Some people are straining themselves. It is not the way to do it. Your face will be so beautiful, dead, no movement. It is dead. Then the mind will be awake. Body is asleep, but mind is awake.

Question: You said these were okay to do at home. Do you recommend any amount of time?

Answer: Do any way you want but emphasize only that line. Do not just do four people. Can you see a straight line? Walk upon it, paint it again, fantastic, this color, that color. Go over it, but do not hurry to reach perfection because then you will leave lots of gaps. In spiritual striving the worst thing is to leave gaps on your path. We will bridge them, bridge them.

Question: What does the vertical line represent and what does the horizontal line represent?

Answer: Vertical and horizontal lines are your right and left brain, are your spirit and matter, are positive and negative energies, are Cosmic Fire and Fohat, millions of things. Which one am I going to tell? It is not important to you. Seventy years I am killing myself to know these things, and in half an hour you cannot empty me. If you try to empty me, you will have a problem.

Good luck! I am so happy you were here. Do not be disappointed. You did not fail anything. You gained. These exercises are very advanced Temple exercises. They will be conquered step by step. There is no hurry in it, and if you hurry it is not good for you. Take it as a child's game.

Next time we will start again with a little review and we will do another symbol.

Summary — *Lesson One*

Close your eyes. Relax.

1. Visualize an equal-armed cross.
2. Visualize a big, flat wall in green or white. Look at it. Touch it with your hands. Feel the texture.
3. Move five feet away and see that a vertical line comes down from top to bottom.
4. Trace the line with chalk or anything in any color you like. Make it 2-3 inches wide. Keep it steady.
5. Put the wall on the floor and have the line on it from top to bottom.
6. Step on the line, and walk to the top. Return and repeat.
7. Walk up the line midway, and see a horizontal line. Now you have a cross.
8. Sit in the center and see both horizontal sides with your eyes.
9. Return to the bottom of the cross and look at it. It is very large and stable. Make it any color you like.
10. Go to the center again and become four people, each going to one end of the cross.
11. Come back to the bottom and open your eyes.

The Art of Visualization

Second Class

If you have questions from the last class you can ask now. How did you do with the exercises? Did you have any successes? Did you have any difficulties? Let us sort it out and clean it.

Question: When a person visualizes, is he actually supposed to see it?

Answer: You are going to see it or imagine it, at least. You are imagining a cross, a big cross, and it is not moving. It is not changing. It is still, and it is the color you want. If you establish that in your mind, you are very successful. Sometimes you cannot see it, but sometimes you can see it. You can see the small one, then blow it out into a big one. Then you walk on it, right and left. Then you go to the center and become four people.

This is a very good exercise and I do not anticipate that you will immediately do it, but a start is something. You can do it until the last day of your life. In that way you gain control over your mind. To control the mind is not easy. As *The Bhagavad Gita* says, the mind is like the wind. How to control that wind? But persistent efforts eventually will bring the reward of controlling that mental substance. That is your victory. Life after life, if every life you gain ten percent victory over it, then twenty, thirty, forty, when you come to fifty percent you will feel that you are your own lord.

Question: Why is it so difficult to remain as one and put ourselves in the four corners?

Answer: It is a fear and identification with your body. Your mental body is very fluidic and not controlled. For many lives you never worked on this. If you work on your arm every day, every life, your arm becomes stronger. It is a matter of exercise. There are no geniuses. There are no trash people. It is all exercise. If you exercise, if you master your bodies, you eventually will be a Master. Our goal is to reach there, no matter how much we failed in this life. Because of some chance, because of the economic, political, and social conditions, the finite ate us. If the finite chews us, we become finite. But now this is a chance. We are flipping a new page. We are starting something which is far away. As the Chinese say, "To walk to the top of the mountain takes one step." Take one step, second step, third step, and you will be getting closer.

As I said many, many times, in spiritual striving there is no hurry. Do not burn yourself. I hurried many times. Instead of going fifty miles per hour, I went five hundred miles per hour and it was bad. So I am telling you from my experience, take it easy and steadily exercise. But one thing is very important. *Do not expect results.* That is the key. If the disciple expects the result, he is frustrated. He has failed. "One week I did it and I cannot see anything. Two weeks I tried and I cannot see it. Throw it out." You should not say that. Say, "I did not succeed today. Tomorrow I will succeed a little more, next day a little more." Sometimes great success comes after you feel that you are failing. This is from experience I am telling you.

You are doing the exercise for three months and one week. You see that it is not working. The cross is going zigzag, turning, disappearing, and you are going in all directions and you do not know what to do. Maybe success is hidden until one week later. I have spoken about *The Bhagavad Gita*, about persistent effort in life and death. Death must not overcome you. You will pass through the door and continue your visualization in astral and mental levels. Teachers will come and teach you. If you learn, then you will come back with tremendous visualization capacities.

Do not be trapped in one life, in sickness, in this or that. It is all in us because we messed in the past and the poison has accumulated in us. We absorbed the poison and it accumulated, so we are sick. It does not matter. We can refine it and clean the way and go.

Question: In the last class when I did the visualization my wall was cracked. What does this mean?

Answer: It is good that you saw it.

Question: I have a question about dividing into four. What does one do with one's individuality, one's eyes, one's ears? Do these divide into four?

Answer: The Self is divisible. You can express yourself in ten, fifteen, or more forms and still be the One Self, several aspects in all the forms of your Self, as the Self.

As far as the cross, it has nothing to do with ego, with yourself. It is the mental plane. The mental plane is ever-flowing substance. It is jerking, turning, going. With willpower you will fix it and say in this substance, "I am creating something substantial, a cross." If you did that, eventually the place that the cross occupied will enlarge, enlarge, and you will conquer the whole mental plane. There is no ego, no self.

Question: Are you the observer watching these four people?

Answer: No, you become four people and each goes to one corner. But you are observing the cross. Imagine there is a cross there. Close your eyes and see it. Can you see it? That is it. If you are observing, you are not doing it. You will split and go. That is the test, but you do not need to do it if you cannot do it because it is far advanced. I gave it for the future.

Question: Can you use this to improve the quality of your meditation?

Answer: As you visualize better, you meditate better. Why? It means your mind is under your control. Meditation means to take the mental body under your control. Ten minutes you are meditating on patience. Okay, you are going to a dance, to a party, and ten minutes are over. "I finished my meditation." It is silly. We are talking here about real things.

I was not serious long ago, but I started slowly, slowly to be serious because time is coming up for you and for me. This is it.

Question: Should these exercises be done with our meditation or at another time?

Answer: Meditation is not connected with it. The difference between meditation and visualization is very great. Meditation is to spread your mental substance into the Divine Mind and fuse with It to take tremendous ideas. Visualization is only subject to the mental plane, lower mental and higher, at least at this stage.

Question: Is it okay to do the mental exercises twice a day?

Answer: Yes. Exercises do not hurt you. There is no danger in doing the exercise except one thing. You must do it in a very relaxed way, not stiffly. Relax and let it come — a cross. I have not seen it yet. Now it came. It is a very nice cross. I did not force it. The mental body is immediately obeying. Later it will turn into a great tool for creativity, rebuilding, and recreating. We are working on it. Not all of us have achieved it, but we are on the way, ten, fifteen, twenty, forty, fifty years.

Close your eyes. We will first of all do the cross. See a big wall and upon it see a big cross. It has no relationship to religion. The cross is not a Christian symbol. The cross is a very ancient symbol. See if you can imagine or totally you are blank, but imagination works in the blankness. You can imagine that you are seeing. Relax and start trying it. Now walk upon it, from north to south, from east to west. Walk on the cross. Look in front of you. You are following the path. It is a pretty big cross.

Now imagine a big wall, a white wall, and put on that wall a little triangle, five inches. Then make it bigger, bigger,

bigger, until the whole wall is a triangle. You are learning a new dance. How difficult is it? Imagine or visualize a big triangle. The top is there, an equal-armed triangle.

Visualize that the left side of the triangle is red. The bottom is blue. The right side is orange. Now try to see these three colors at the same time. You will love it eventually. It is fantastic — red, blue, orange.

First see every side separately. The left side is red. You can detect that, one line. Then see the bottom line, which is blue. Then see the right line, which is orange.

Is there any success? Fantastic. It is so beautiful. A man was saying to me, "T., I do not know what to do with my time. I am bored. I am lonely." I said, "Sit and visualize." "What does that mean?" he asked. "Son of a gun, you have so much to do with yourself. Time is given to you. Use it." What is loneliness? We have every minute to work on ourselves.

Now again, let us start with red. A First Ray individual can easily see a red line. Then you come to the base line which is blue. A Second Ray man can easily see blue. Now try to see the whole picture — red, blue, and orange. Even if you cannot see, pretend you are imagining it. It is a progress. A Third Ray man can easily see orange.

We did this one year in the Temple. At first I was so bored. After three months I got very serious and it started. It is so beautiful.

Question: When I see the three colors at one time, it feels like the inside of my mind is expanding outwardly.

Answer: That is it. Form does something. Form crystallizes the energy. Color expands the mind because color is related to many levels. What are we doing? We are making the triangle red. Red is going to the Atmic Plane. Blue is going to the Intuitional Plane. Orange is going to the Monadic Plane. That is very good that you felt it. It is expansion. I mean, you cannot pay enough to know that this is a masterpiece for you. Reading is okay, meditation is okay, but beyond that this must be done in the meantime.

Now let us do it again. On the wall is a one inch triangle, very small. Make it two inches with the colors, three inches, four inches, one yard, two yards. See what is happening to your mental body, ten yards, a huge triangle. Now see the colors. You will do it. Do not worry. Worry must not enter into your mind and hurry must not enter. This is a "take it easy exercise." Every day do it for five minutes, ten minutes, half an hour. Eventually you will see it in front of your eyes like on a television screen.

Now shift the triangle and bring the point down and the base up. It is almost one yard. Now can you rotate it clockwise, from right to left as if it were spinning on a nail? First it is a slow speed, very slow, then faster, faster, and you will see a circle when it is rotating. Now stop it. Sometimes you cannot stop its turning, but you must stop it. Now turn from left to right, counter-clockwise. Stop it. The point is above. The base is down. Look at the colors. Okay, report to me.

You see, how many books you have read or know is not too important until you actualize yourself. To actualize means to have control over your mental plane.

Question: I was getting so relaxed that my hands tingled.

Answer: Of course it is very nice. It is a relaxant because the mind is finding its real role. Our mind is chaotic, nervous, irritable. When you do these exercises, you are relaxed. What you must do is to do them in a really relaxed way. No tension, no tension at all, and no hurrying, and no expectation. You must follow these three rules. Go sit under a tree and say, "I am doing visualization." Sometimes you can do it open-eyed. I look at a white wall and in two minutes a triangle comes — red, blue, orange. Now I am spinning it. You see it on the wall, and if in the future you want to see your Master, you see Him on the wall. You visualize His face and He is there.

Twice I gave in my books how to come in contact with your Master. But it is so advanced that no one has tried or dared. I put it there for a future record so that you can do it. Do not waste your time reading other books. I am telling you, do not waste your time. If you assimilate my one hundred and fifty books, they will take you to Shamballa. You do not need other books. Do not waste your time. I sincerely tell it, not because I have an ego. I do not have an ego.

Question: Can you do this with your eyes open?

Answer: Yes, of course. If you are capable of doing it, why not? But if you do it with eyes open, you may be interrupted by various shadows, various forms. Everything may interfere. But if you are concentrated, it is fantastic.

Question: Does the addition of color create a desire for movement? I wanted to spin it even before you said to spin it.

Answer: Color already spins it. When you put in color, the spinning starts because it is tied to three levels. This exercise is tied to three levels. But you must be able to stop the spinning, retard it, speed it, then stop it again so that your mental capacity is up-to-date. Sometimes you spin it and it spins forever and drives you crazy. You are going to stop it.

Close your eyes. See a plate that is put vertically and put one ball on it and see how the ball is going down. The ball is going down. Take it and put it up again and down it goes. Put it up again and it is going down. Now put it again and half way stop it mentally. See if you can do it. Those who stopped it, make it come back up, not down. Try again. Put the ball and let it go close, close, close to the bottom and stop it like an electrical switch. Then let it climb up. Now do something difficult. Put the ball up again and make it go sixty miles per hour, then five miles, then two miles, one mile, slowly. Then it is at the bottom. Make it go up one mile per hour, two miles, three miles, fifty miles per hour, reach to the top.

I am giving this additional exercise just to show that it is hard to control the mind. I wrote many, many exercises, and you can find them in other books. The ball is going like this. Stop it, hurry, stop, go back, faster. What your mind is doing is controlling a thoughtform. No other progress of humans is equal to this because you are becoming mental people — not physical, emotional people, but mental people. You are getting victory over yourselves.

Question: When we were doing the triangles with the colors, the blue became just like looking at blue through a church window. It became brilliant and beautiful.

Answer: It means that the corresponding level in you is very active, very awake. If it is all blurred, it means the corresponding levels are not working.

Question: Are there any situations or conditions of our bodies in which it is dangerous for us to do these exercises and we must stop for awhile?

Answer: There is no danger. Immediately when you are emotional, immediately when you are lonely, immediately when you are this or that, close your eyes, relax, and do these exercises. They will uplift you, make you to conquer an emotional situation. Now I am here. Do you see emotion in me? I am dying. I have liver cancer, hopeless, but I keep talking to you. Can you imagine that? I ate peanuts when I was four years old. The peanut oil went to my liver and started cancer. It was growing in me for eighty years. If They want to heal it, They will heal it. If They do not want, good-bye.

Be well, and be faithful to the group. Cooperate, harmonize, and be in self-denial. If there is no self-denial in you, you failed. Have self-denial in everything. Do not push yourself. It is self-denial. The overall interest is important. I built this sanctuary. I will come back and build the university. Do not worry. Life after life, in life and in death we are saying, "I will serve you, Lord." That is the key, in life and in death, seriously. To serve, you need tools. This is one of the greatest tools in your hand. Try to visualize. Try to conquer these things.

Let us start again. See a triangle, five inches big approximately. See the colors. Make it a little bigger. Cover the whole wall with a nice triangle, an artistic triangle, in red, blue, and orange. Relax and let it come there. Suddenly it hits, one second. Then you have a success, but first in creative imagination, second in visualization. Now make the triangle into three pieces. Break it. Put the right side right, left side left, bottom down. Now this is interesting. Let them unite in one second. Let them separate. Make them fifteen feet apart from each other, and then order them in your mind to come together. Here, they unite.

Do it again. Take the left piece and see that it is red. Examine it. It is a red piece. Throw it. Now look at the bottom which is blue, a nice blue. Then see the right side, orange. Now snap them together immediately. Electronically they come together. Okay, open your eyes.

Now to facilitate your visualization you can take a pad and take a crayon and draw these things. It is spinning. Then it is breaking. Then it is coming back. Your mind must be occupied with that form. Then go to the cross. Do these together so that your mind visually is impressed, or put a cross there and look at it. Daily look ten times at the cross, the triangle. Look at them. It helps very, very much because from outside they are impressed on your brain. This is an easy method that you can use.

Do not forget the ball. Down, stop, down, stop, up, stop, up, stop, up, stop. It is such a fantastic exercise. If you succeed a little, your evolution will go five hundred years ahead.

Question: Is it important that these shapes are geometric, regular in form?

Answer: Yes.

Question: I am thinking, let me decorate this ball with flowers and things.

Answer: The mind is monkeying with you, side-tracking you. That is one of the things that you are going to forbid.

Your duty is a triangle, control of a triangle, control of a cross. The next time we are going to do a sphere or circle. It is great fun.

Now you will take this and work sixty, seventy years, as long as you live, but do not expect quick results. I was very bad in visualization because I am First Ray. First Ray souls cannot visualize. I said, "I am going to break it." It took sixty years to break. Then suddenly I can see everywhere what I want to see. It is so fantastic that without vanity or ego I will tell you that if I work in those levels, I can give you other books and writings that are a thousand times more advanced, but why to give? That is my agony, my suffering. I would like everybody to know what I know.

When my Father used to take me to parties, they had lots of nuts at those parties, rotten nuts, good nuts, nice nuts, and my favorite, peanuts. Whatever I found beautiful there I wanted my sisters to have. So I put in my pocket sweets and different things so that I share them with my sisters. I was not happy to be there except when I took some goodies and brought them to my sisters. "Sisters, look, nuts, look, bonbons, lots of things." They were so fantastic, dozens of kinds of nuts, sugars, and so on.

Now I am giving these things as a life exercise. Go home and draw a cross and add as much information as you can remember on it. Then do the triangle. What did he say? He said this. He said that. Then he brought the ball, changed the speed, made it stop, and go back. Then what did he do? He broke the lines of the triangle and united them. Write the exercises down on a special paper, in a special book, so that when we finish you have it. Good luck. You have fifty years to work on it.

Do not forget this. Visualization helps your mental level to digest whatever you are hearing and reading.

Without visualization there is no digestion. It stays book knowledge, and you do not like it. Books, books, books. Eventually you get crazy because you did not digest them. That is why visualization opens the mind, cleans the mind, exercises the muscle to digest, to assimilate, and when you are reading a book, you read one little paragraph and say, "Wow, what a beautiful thing is this." Then you accumulate so much wisdom and beauty that you give it through your writings, through your life, your relationships.

Question: What does it mean if you can see more easily with your eyes open instead of closed?

Answer: There are two kinds of people, introverts and extroverts. This is in psychology. Assagioli and many other psychologists defined that. Some people are introverts. They see inside. Some people are extroverts. They see outside. My Teacher, who was an extrovert, could not see with his eyes closed, but he could see anything with his eyes open. And the interesting thing is that I used to sit by him when he was exercising by building a shape. All my hairs would stand up. One day he visualized the Master.

I am very lucky that I passed through these experiences and brought them to you. How much did you receive? It was thirty-five percent. Sixty-five percent you are going to bury with T. Next time. Next time we will come again. I will meet you. We have millions of friends. Imagine how many lives we lived and how many groups we formed. They are there on the mental level, astral level, intuitional level, scattered all over the world. Now how to bring them together in a nice way so that they do not eat each other, fight each other with ego, vanity, I am big, you are small, I am chairman, you are trash, and so on. Self-denial is the foundation of success.

You can visualize with your eyes open, but you are going to visualize by looking at a blank, white wall. Look at it and start visualizing, but you are not going to blink. My Teacher used to stay half an hour, and His eyes were wide open. I can stay half an hour, no tears, nothing. You bring all that energy into your eyes.

Do these exercises every day to prepare yourself for the next class. Good luck to all of you.

Summary — *Lesson Two, part one*

1. Repeat the first lesson's exercise.
2. Stop a few minutes.
3. Visualize a big white wall and place a little five inch triangle on it.
4. Enlarge the triangle until the whole wall is filled with the triangle.
5. Make the left side of the triangle the color red, the bottom blue, and the right side orange.
6. See each side separately. Then put them together.
7. Repeat from step 2 again until you are able to stabilize it.
8. Shift the triangle to point it down.
9. Rotate it clockwise from right to left, first at a slow pace, then faster. Stop the rotation. Repeat the rotation counter-clockwise. Put the point up again. Observe the colors.
10. Take a deep breath.

— Lesson Two, part two

Mental control exercise

1. Visualize a plate standing vertically.
2. Put a ball on it and watch it go down. Put it up, and let it go down. Stop it from going down. Repeat several times until you are able to stop the ball and make it go up or down at will. Let the ball fall at progressively faster speeds, then up again slowly and then faster.
3. Take a deep breath.

— Lesson Two, part three

1. Start again with the triangle and see it as five inches.
2. See the colors — red, blue, orange.
3. Make it bigger, covering the whole wall.
4. Make the triangle into three pieces, separating it. Then unite the pieces. Make the pieces fifteen feet apart from each other. Unite them. Repeat.
5. Look at each individual piece with its color. Snap them together.
6. Take a deep breath.

Note: To help your visualization, you can draw these forms, put them upon a wall, and look at them occasionally.

The Art of Visualization

Third Class

Last time we finished a little triangle. Today we are going to do a circle, but for the first four or five minutes let us do the triangle.

Close your eyes and see a big wall and upon the wall the triangle, a big triangle — red, blue, and orange. Try to see it, first one side, then the bottom, then the other side. If you cannot see it, imagine it. Imagination is the door to visualization.

I am going to give you time. Make the red a nice red, then the blue and red together, and then see the red, blue, and orange together. The triangle is now complete. You try to see it, to imagine it.

Now start from the orange side. See how the orange and red are different. In your mind the red will make the difference. Orange is different from the red. See how different it is. See blue with orange. Look what is happening and add the red.

Put a nail in the center of the triangle and with your hand turn it. Give it a kick. Let it turn clockwise, first slowly, then speedily, speedily, then more speedily. Do it again.

Now do it anti-clockwise. Turn it twenty times and stop it. Now the triangle is turning anti-clockwise. Make it turn twenty-five times. Then stop it. See if you can stop it in your imagination or in your visualization. Then continue again to make it revolve clockwise. See if you can discriminate the colors. Do this for five minutes.

This exercise looks like a hallucination but it has a profound influence on your mind and brain. If this is taught to the children, your children will never fall into trouble and you will never have mental trouble. This gives you mental sanity, destroys in the mental level lots of mess, collected mess. From life to life, from day to day, it cleans, it throws out, it kills them. What a blessing.

Then the mental plane reflects on to the astral plane. It kills lots of things there and prepares you to be very honest and direct in your relationships and not to hide any microbes in your being, in your psyche. This cleans you and breaks you out. It is very, very important. People can hide from people, but they cannot hide from themselves. This clarifies, cleans, makes you direct and pure. Do it always if you can, and if you have little children, teach them.

Now we are going to close our eyes again. This time you are seeing the triangle, but around it a circle. Imagine or visualize it. You are going to imagine again the triangle and around it a circle. The circle is white, pure white, snow white. Start again, a triangle, three colors. Repeat them always so that they are impressed in your mind. Put a circle around it, a very thick circle.

Now we have a challenge here, and this is very esoteric and higher psychic. Look at the triangle that is turning in the circle clockwise and see the circle turning anti-clockwise.

Now there is ten minutes for you to do that.

Struggle, fail, be successful. Keep your mind active. If you fail any moment, start from the beginning. Do not be discouraged because these exercises are very ancient and they require years and lives. A little grasp is fine. You can turn the triangle with your hand and the circle with the other hand, or mentally you can direct it. Mental direction is more powerful than the hands. You can focus on the mental direction later, but try to do it with your hands. It is a little tricky for beginners.

Fantastic.

Some people are doing good. Some people are not concentrating. One of you is not doing it. You are hallucinating.

Build upon it — triangle, then circle. One is turning clockwise. One is turning anti-clockwise. Everybody overall is doing not bad. One of you is squeezing herself. Relax.

Now as the circle is turning anti-clockwise, imagine that the triangle is evaporating. You have only a white circle turning anti-clockwise. Now enter into that circle and see that it is becoming a sphere and you are sitting in the sphere. Feel the walls, how they are electrical and psychic, beautiful. Imagine the sphere is expanding, becoming two, three feet away from your body. See that it is not hollow. It is filled with psychic energy which you are absorbing. It is penetrating every part of you, cleansing, charging, healing.

Get out of the sphere and put it on your head. See that there are rainbow colors in it, shining on your head. It is so beautiful. Now you started to do that. Very good. I am giving time to make you repeat, repeat, repeat, eventually to visualize better. If I do not talk, do not stop. Do it.

Five minutes more.

Feel the sphere on your head in rainbow colors. And now see in it a little triangle and at the center of the triangle a little cross. Now let me see if you can do it. Imagine.

Let us stop. Did you have fun? It was so beautiful.

Question: When you put the sphere on your head, how is it placed?

Answer: A sphere is a sphere, a ball. How do you put a big ball on your head? That is it, like this, a big ball on your head, a big balloon. It is not entering inside. It is resting on your head.

Question: I have a headache. Am I doing something wrong?

Answer: No, a headache is very good because it is cleaning some crystallizations. It is very, very good. I wish I had a headache. It is not enough what I have!

Question: Is the rainbow radiating out?

Answer: You can imagine it any way you want, a rainbow all around it or inside it or outside it. Beautiful. It is what your artistic ability can cultivate.

Question: What did you say to put in the center of the triangle?

Answer: I said that there is a sphere and bring a triangle into the sphere red, blue, orange, and at the middle put a little cross.

Question: Most of the time we are visualizing outside of us. Is it all right to visualize this formation inside our head?

Answer: No, I am glad you asked. If I am seeing the sphere here, you are in the sphere. You are imagining everything in the sphere, not bringing it inside. If it is turning, it is not turning inside. It is turning on the top of your head so that you detach yourself and learn absolute detachment in the future.

These are profound exercises, and if I have more life I will give you every three months these kind of things that will enhance your evolution. This is very, very important because this is a part of your actualization process. You can read one book, okay, very good, very nice. It does not help until you do these things because these exercises are really changing the substance of your mind and letting you have control over it. You do not know how important these are.

One day I asked a yogi who was like a skeleton sitting near a cave, "What do you do two, three hours sitting like that?" He said, "I visualize." "What do you visualize?" I asked. "Oh, every day something else. For example, I visualize a tree, a beautiful tree, and every branch becomes light. Every branch becomes a different kind of animal. Then a symphony starts in it. Then the animals turn around the tree branches. Then a branch becomes a nation, and so on." He went on and on because in visualization there is no end if you once start seeing it.

The yogi was slowly, slowly progressing, and in this progression of visualization he was manifesting his psychic abilities, how much he can see, how much he can do, how complicated is the tree, how much more he can complicate the tree. Once you see it, it is a different phenomenon. For example, you can visualize ten girls. You look at them and they are dressed fantastically. The music starts and you make them dance. Look now. There is color, music, movement. You make a fantastic dance and improve it, improve it, and eventually it becomes such a dance, magnetic, psychic, and then you bring it into actualization, into a real dance. You do not form from outside. You form first in your mind.

Question: How long can we do this every day?

Answer: You can do it from half an hour to two hours, if you have time. The first command is not to tense your body but to be in total relaxation. Sometimes you think that when you are doing these exercises you need to tense your eyebrows, or eyes, or ears. It is not that. Sometimes you hold your chair and cling to it. This is tension. Your body is going to sleep. The body is dead. The mind is working. The mind now looks. I let it go, and a cross comes and the triangle comes. Even my eyes are a little open. Then the circle comes.

Then I can do another thing. I take a song. One sound is for the cross. Another sound is for the triangle. Another sound is for the circle. I build chords and I listen. Visualization is not only for the eye. All our senses visualize. The ears visualize. I did not have time to teach these things because you did not show too much interest in classes. We lost lots of time. We lost at least fifty dances. Those dances, if I organized them, you would flip out. You are going to organize that very complicated mechanism, and if you do not do it immediately, do it again, and do not say, "I cannot do it." You cannot do it now, but you can do it in the future.

A baby takes the pencil and says, "I cannot write," but then fifty years later he becomes an author. Say you cannot do this visualization now, but you can learn it little by little, little by little, and then change your senses. There is visualization by ear. Now how am I visualizing by ear? I am listening to music — "O Living Flame." I am really hearing it. That is visualization. Then you make it two, three voices. Wow! Then you make it four voices — bass, tenor, contralto, soprano — that is the ear. Then do the smell.

Close your eyes. Smell a jasmine. See if you can smell it. Change it into a rose. That is easy. I am not going to practice this because it is very advanced, but it gives an example that visualization is the wrong word. Every sense can visualize. Touch can visualize. Taste can visualize. Taste a lemon in your mouth. Immediately your saliva starts. Then taste something else, a steak you are eating! Every sense has visualization.

Now scientifically, if I have an Ashram, which means really, really dedicated students, then I would teach them visualization in all five senses. Then I would connect them into the Intuition. They would be masterpieces.

Look, from my little viewpoint what I did for you: the Agoura property, fourteen acres, beautiful. Seven acres here, buildings, books, music, songs. How did they come? They all came from visualization. Is it finished? No, it has just started. You are going to continue and prove that you are disciples. You can do it. Now Mommy died, Daddy died. You are ten years old. You are going to take care of yourself with the best of your knowledge, utilizing the *Leadership* Volumes, I to V, and other books, creating an expansion so that the Aquarian Educational Group becomes a field of service to humanity. We are not working for ourselves. That must change in your consciousness.[1]

Question: Was it inherent in this color triangle, once you brought it into formation, that sound and fragrance come into existence at the same time, or do you create sounds and colors?

Answer: No, you do not create. You follow the instructions, and that triad reflects the Spiritual Triad and the circle reflects the Monad and different things. The bottom line is very deep. I cannot give it to you now. But slowly do it. Do not jump to the circle if you could not do the cross — years, years, years, the cross. Crucify yourself on the cross. Then slowly go to the triangle. Then slowly go to the circle. In the fourth and last lesson we will see what we can do. But until you come there, you try at home as much as you can.

One thing I am going to repeat always. Never think that you are failing, your mind is failing, you are failing because you cannot see. It impresses slowly. If you do a circle in your mental substance, it goes like the waves in the ocean. You do again. It stays one minute, then goes. You do again, it stays a few minutes. This is it. Do not give up. Eventually the mental substance says, "There is something going on here," and gets condensed and enters under your control.

---

[1]The Aquarian Educational Group was founded by the author. One Center is in Agoura, California and the other in Sedona, Arizona.

Question: What is the difference when you are trying to visualize something with your different senses, than remembering. For example, when you say to visualize the smell of the jasmine, if you have smelled the jasmine, you know what it smells like. How is the memory interacting with the process of the visualization?

Answer: The memory is a little help, but if you lean on the memory you cannot develop visualization. You start with a memory that you have smelled a jasmine. Yesterday some lady gave you jasmine. Then leave it. Then start to smell it. Are you really smelling jasmine now? Yes, it is so interesting. You will literally smell it, which means literally you are seeing the form. They are correspondences, but it is a very complicated science. What we are seeing is the surface. The iceberg is miles down.

Question: If these headaches get strong, should you do it for a little less time?

Answer: Do you still have a headache? Did you drink wine? It will vanish. It may not be visualization. It can be some physiological reasons that you must discriminate very sharply. For example, ladies have different phases in their lives that affect them. If you have your period, you must not be doing it if it is affecting you. For a few days take a leave, but in those few days you can take a crayon and make a circle, triangle, crosses. These must come to your mind. You must visualize them.

When I was doing these things in the monastery, one of my Teachers came into my room. There were fifty triangles, ten crosses, all of them right there so every minute I would see them. Then by seeing, seeing, they are in me now. I can visualize them.

This is the spiritual path. You are taking a virtue and assimilating that virtue, directness, honesty, purity, not lying, not deceiving, not pretending — oh, how beautiful.

Then there are other methods. For example, I said a cross. What experience do you have with a cross? This is if we have time. You will dig into your memories and bring from the subconscious or higher consciousness memories that are painful or very joyful. What memories do you have? For example, one day a priest hit my head with a cross. I still feel the pain. Now there is this kind of memory. You had a cross your friend gave to you. You have millions of memories.

Then there are triangles. I remember one day a friend brought a package that was wrapped and gave it to me. It was a triangle with a diamond in the middle. This is a triangle memory. There are other triangles.

Then you come to the circle. Circles are in abundance. I used to have an iron circle and would run after it. It was so much fun in the old country. You have a little iron like this and you push it and it goes and I would run after it. There are sad stories about it and good stories. Now eventually you must pull these things out of your memory bank, arrange, integrate, and computerize them, and then let them vanish.

I am showing you the possibility of expansion, so that you do not think that I am just giving visualization.

Question: In doing this in group formation, does it help us in any way to make breakthroughs?

Answer: I will tell you something. My health was the worst from six years on. I was always sick. My Mother said, "Sick, sick, sick, I am sick of it." It was my stomach, my heart, my lungs. The only thing that helped me was visualization. Then when I was forty, forty-five, I grabbed it, and here I am eighty. Look, with liver cancer I am coming and giving you lectures. You would be scared to death in your bed. Do you realize that? You do not. Every lecture is worth more than ten thousand dollars. Who cares if I am sick. It does not exist even. In this attitude we overcome our weaknesses and do not bow to sickness.

Actually, eventually, you will realize that you are as pure as the snow. It is all the body. It is all trash. It is all time. Let it go. But of course this is easy to say. When you are sick, it is not so easy because we are identified with our bodies.

Question: Do we always wait at least two hours after eating?

Answer: Yes, always two hours. It is imperative because this visualization takes energy from the stomach, liver, and intestines. Do not eat and start. You are ruining yourself. Wait for two hours to pass. Pick a nice time, the afternoon, at sunset when you are happy, when you have finished eating two hours ago, or do it at night. It is a pleasant game. Do not force yourself on it. It will force itself on you eventually. When you are sitting on the bank of the river, and you ask, "What am I doing? I am looking at the lakes, doing this and that. Let me do visualization." Close your eyes, or look at the river and visualize. If you are an extrovert you can do it. Do not lose your time. Be after visualization, and if time is given to me I really wish to give you all other senses. Now you have a little understanding of the importance of visualization.

In the past, occasionally I gave in the seminars visualization exercises, mental exercises that were the beginning to make your mind fit for them, but I did not see devotion. Fifty people must come and say, "We are ready to do these things." I did not see it. Three people come. Five people come. Ten people do not come. The next time they are sick. The next time they are at a party. The next time they are jumping, drinking. "I cannot do that." Then you lose the opportunity. Later you will understand that I was an opportunity. I do not say this with vanity and ego, but you did not profit from me as much as you could have. Now try to profit from the books.

Summary — *Lesson Three, part one*

1. For five minutes repeat the triangle exercise. Look at each color separately, then together.
2. Put a nail in the center of the triangle and turn it clockwise, slowly, then faster.
3. Turn it counter-clockwise twenty times and stop it. Again turn it counter-clockwise twenty-five times and stop it. Repeat, turning it clockwise. Do this for five minutes, trying always to discriminate the colors.
4. Take a break.

— *Lesson Three, part two*

1. Begin again with the triangle in three colors. Put a white circle around it. Make the lines very thick.
2. See the triangle turning clockwise and the circle turning counter-clockwise.
3. Do this for ten minutes. If you fail, stop and repeat

from the start of this exercise. Build each piece until you can stabilize it. Stay relaxed.

4. As the circle is turning counter-clockwise, make the triangle disappear and only the turning circle remains.
5. Enter into the circle and make it a sphere. Sit in it. Feel the walls. Let it expand 2-3 feet away from your body. See it filled with psychic energy which you are absorbing. It is cleansing you, charging and healing you.
6. Get out of the sphere and put it on your head. See it with rainbow colors, shining on your head.
7. Keep repeating until you have it. Do this for five minutes.
8. Keeping the sphere on your head with the rainbow colors, add a little triangle at the middle, and on the triangle, a cross.
9. Work on this so that it is clear. Build and rebuild in the same sequence — sphere, triangle, cross.
10. Take a rest.

— Lesson Three, part three

Every sense has visualization. You can try visualizing with other senses.

The Art of Visualization

Fourth Class

Now close your eyes. See a square box. Open it and enter into it and close it. Feel the walls, right, left, down, up. Count how many walls you have. Just feel them. Get out of the box and look at the square box. Make it bigger and bigger until it is quite big. Make it smaller, smaller, until it is one inch. Can you imagine now, nicely? Try it.

Visualize a one inch square box. Make it all yellow. Make it yellow and white, one side white, one side yellow, and take it in your hand and look at it. Make it all red. Take the square box and nail it on the wall. Now can you see a square on the wall? Take the cross and nail it upon the box. Now you have a red box and a cross on it, let us say a white cross. Now put around the square and cross a triangle. The triangle is all blue. There is a blue triangle, a white cross, and behind it is a red box. Visualize them if you can. If you cannot visualize, just imagine it, but let me see you fight with it. Take your time. Your success depends on striving. The red square box, white cross, and blue triangle are all together.

Go very slowly and do it again and again until it becomes a little more clear. That little improvement is what you need. Now see around the blue triangle a circle, a violet, fiery circle. Push the square far away, the cross far away, the triangle far away, and see how they look in the frame of the circle. Okay, you will have five minutes rest.

Give me some reports.

Question: My picture, when I project it, only seems to go to the right, never to the left. I try to put it in the middle, but it keeps going to the right.

Answer: It is because your left brain is working harder. There is no balance. You are going to balance it. It takes time. These exercises are brain adjustments. You are adjusting things there, brain and mental body. Sometimes the mental body and brain are not coordinated. The mental body sees the triangle, while the brain looks at it as a fluctuation. So it means that there is some lack of coordination. Actually these are very, very advanced psychiatrical, psychological exercises to find out what is going on in you, not to take your brain picture but to give it a little exercise and know what is going on in your mind. If you are totally coordinated, mentally and brain wise, you will see the picture as it is, but we are on the way. Nobody can reach to that perfection at once. If in the past you did not work for it, it is almost impossible for you to do something. But if you take five steps, that is the beginning. No one is expecting miracles, that you really see. Sometimes you see part of it. Sometimes you see one symbol. Then you lose it. Then it blurs out, then imagination starts, then visualization starts, and then again it fades away. Now what is it? It is the fluctuation of the mental substance. If we learn how to substantiate and make it concrete in that level, our mental body will be able to do great miracles.

This is not the case for us in that degree, but we are on the way. When else are we going to start it?

Question: Is there an emotional visualization?

Answer: If emotion enters into visualization, the visualization becomes emotional and devotional, a worshipful object, and you do not want to prostrate the higher ideas, the higher visions, by bringing them into the emotional and etheric planes. Also, it can cause lots of trouble for you. A mental picture is a fiery picture, whether it is totally built or not built. Immediately when you imagine, you visualize, it is in your mental plane. The mental plane has seven levels. In the highest level, it is really there. In the lowest level, there is a mixing of your mental hallucinations and different things. It is in fluctuation. For example, you throw an object into the water and it goes down, it becomes invisible, but if you bring that fiery substance to the emotional plane, it may conflict and create lots of emotional troubles. These are warnings that people do not know. They say, "Visualize." Okay, but what is happening?

Question: When you say to open our eyes, I still see those images with open eyes. Is this bad or good?

Answer: It is good. Take a baby or take a man who is going to try to learn the violin. I learned the violin. I played so beautifully sometimes, but it took a long time for me to adjust my fingers, my brain, read the notes, and then adjust this hand, that hand, the brain. Visualization, aspiration came slowly together, but it took many years! You will not believe it if I tell you. I used to do three hours of practice every day. My Mother used to close her ears and run from the house. I made such noise that I drove her crazy. Then I went to practice on the roof. She still heard. . . . I did not know where to go. I did everything possible not to miss three hours of practice.

I remember the Hungarian Rhapsody. I heard somebody playing it. He played it so beautifully. I went crazy. I said, "I am going to learn that." I played every measure fifty times, then fifty times the second measure with the first measure, then the third measure with the first and second measure. I did it! When everything was finished, I knew it by heart.

Do you know how many times I did it? If you make a mathematical calculation you will see, but I did it. I was frustrated sometimes. I wanted to break the violin. "You son of a gun, you are not playing right." I was not playing right, not the violin, but when I finished, I played it, and my Father came and hugged me. He said, "You make the chairs, the furniture to cry."

So the matter is effort, striving, doing it again and again without giving up. You can say that this is the life's goal and eventually you are going to do it — not doing it one day and three days not doing it. You are going to do it every day ten minutes, fifteen minutes, half an hour. When you have time, instead of gossip, slander, and so on, or telephone conversations or stupid things, you sit there and do these exercises.

"I am lonely." Do a visualization exercise and you will see that loneliness disappears, really disappears. I am a human being. I became many times severely lonely, I mean, desperate. But when I started visualization, it disappeared. I had something to do. When you do visualization, and you see these objects with their color and form, they become transmitters of higher ideas, visions, and revelations, and you live in a life of glory and beauty through your visualization.

Have you read the book *Thought and the Glory of Thinking*? It is the result of visualization. You cannot take out from that book one word, one sentence. It is a diamond. Are you reading it or waiting for the next life? At least say, "Every day I am going to read one page." Sometimes one page is too much. Half a page is okay. Some of you may have pride, and you do not see what it is.

Question: How do you know when your visualization is becoming emotional?

Answer: You feel it. For example, let us say that you are looking at a sphere. It suddenly changes to a ball. Then you find yourself in a tennis court playing tennis with the ball and you are becoming angry, you are becoming anxious, you are hating people, this or that. It went down. Through association, visualization objects degenerate.

These are fantastic ideas. These symbols — square, cross, triangle, circle — eventually turn into transmitters. Each symbol is an extension of the Intuitional Plane. That is why studying and meditating about the symbols and visualizing the symbols make an access to the Intuitional Plane — every symbol. This is the heavy part of the lecture. Then in the Intuitional Plane, an intuitional form is formed. It radiates to different layers, different people, different centers, and it becomes a radio station bringing you ideas, beautiful ideas. If you are doing a painting, do visualization for a few minutes and you will see what your paintings will be. Immediately your paintings become two, three, four dimensional. You say, "What am I going to do now? It is becoming so beautiful."

Eventually the destination of disciples is not worship but entering into the subjective world, the world of energies, forces, and currents. You are going to enter it. Thirty-five years went by like quick-silver. I tried to hold it with my fingers. It disappeared. Later, visualization becomes tremendous control over the physical, emotional, and mental planes. We did not reach there, but we are going to reach, this life or two lives later. Two lives later, when we become an Arhat or a Master, we will tell our bodies to be masterpieces and they are immediately going to obey because the body is created by thought.

Question: Is there any danger in visualizing just as you fall into sleep, as you are going to sleep?

Answer: Yes, there is danger in visualizing and entering into sleep because you do not know where you are going. If you are going to the mental plane, fantastic, but if you are going to the etheric or astral planes it is worse. You sleep and think it is sleep. But where are you? If you have an experience one day to see how people sleep and what they do after sleep — some go to cabarets, some go to prostitutes, some go to drinking, some make money, cheat. Somebody builds, builds, builds. Other people geometrize. Other people write symphonies. Sleep is sleep, but where is your consciousness entering?

Question: Did you once say not to do visualization after ten o'clock in the evening?

Answer: Yes, I said it. After ten o'clock for most of us, I can say ninety-eight percent, the brain is tired. You must not force your brain. If your brain wants to, okay, but after ten o'clock it is tired. Actually, real disciples sleep at ten o'clock because there is Ashram business to attend to.

Now, again, we are seeing a red box on the wall. By the way, did you see how I arranged the sequence of symbols? If in any way you use these symbols in the wrong sequence, you create upheaval. For example, if you did a circle and printed on it a big triangle, it is involutionary. You are retrogressing. You did something wrong. It is retrogression because symbols are energy sources. You are reversing the plan. You are reversing the process.

First, do the square. After that the cross. The cross is more advanced than the square. Then there is the triangle. The triangle is more advanced than the square and cross. Then there is the sphere or circle. If you visualize it in the wrong way, you are in trouble.

I was in a psychiatrist's room once. Several people were doing visualization. First they were starting with a circle, then a cross, then a triangle, ending with the square. I said, "This is no good." They asked, "What is no good? They are just symbols." "What are symbols?" Well, they did not hear me. I did not talk with them.

Close your eyes. See a red box on the wall. This time I am giving you a little more time. Do not be discouraged. Even if you do not see anything, you are thinking and thinking and doing it. There is a red box. I am seeing it. It is nailed to a wall. Now I am nailing upon it a cross. Fantastic. The cross is white. The square is red. Look how much you can do it. Now bring around it a triangle, a blue triangle. Try to see the three of them. It is very beautiful. Through the triangle you see the cross and the square. Now you have a circle around them and the circle is violet colored. It is not moving yet. Now what are you going to do. Like a camera, you are going to push the square far, far, and then bring it forward, take it far, and bring it forward.

Try to see the colors now, one by one, then all together. Repeat.

Relax your eyebrows. Your neck and eyebrows must be totally relaxed. Also pay attention to your teeth. Teeth must be relaxed as well as your tongue.

Now see a red box. Go and touch it. Examine it. Is it becoming a little real? Yes? Now take a white cross and nail it upon the red box and touch it. Watch your fingers, feel it, see it, touch it. Now put on the blue triangle and go over it with your finger. Look how it feels. Now see them all together — blue triangle, white cross, red box — and now you add the circle. The circle is really a sphere, but it is so transparent that you see the circle and then through the circle the other objects. When you finish, you open your eyes and rub your forehead and eyebrows.

Give me a report. Who saw it? Who did a nice imagination? Who had fluctuations? It is okay. It is part of the game. You cannot swim immediately. They throw you into the water and you do anything stupid to save yourself. This is just like a game.

Question: I could not move the box, the square. It kept turning, so it was sort of rebelling, refusing to obey my will.

Answer: It means that your reasoning and logic are not working under your direction. It is psychological. When you cannot hold the square, your reasoning, your logic are fluctuating. Your mind is fluctuating. It is true, when you sincerely accept it and look at it. Your reasoning and logic are fluctuating. So it is a way to find out what is going on inside with visualization.

Question: When you are doing the visualization, how important is your breathing?

Answer: Before visualization you take three long breaths. Then you forget about it. It goes right automatically. But you must give the first impulse. Sometimes your breathing is very bad. It does not allow you to see it. If it is calm and peaceful breathing, then you visualize better.

Question: Do the colors, the purple, the violet, the blue, do they have different vibrations? Does one of them feel like fire, more potent in some different way?

Answer: Each color is energy. That is why you must be able to mix the colors. Great artists are masters of the color symphony. For example, in the music you cannot mix this note with that note. There is a regular, instinctive decision you can make on how to build that music. The color is the same. It is very important. If you use two colors that are antagonistic to each other, these symbols negate each other.

Question: What is the impact when you take a circle and then turn it into a cylinder or turn it into a sphere and give it volume as opposed to a flat image? Does that have an affect upon us?

Answer: No, it is a game that you are playing, and eventually you will find the best way to do it.

Question: At first there was just a whole rosy glow. I really had to work to bring the red box in. Other times I did not have that problem.

Answer: Fifty years ago I said, "It is all a black wall. I cannot see anything." Now it is not so because I worked on it. If I did not have this group, I would be a Master in this life. But I postponed my evolution. Twenty-four hours I work for the group. All these letters, lessons, instructions are not done during office hours. I am going home and working more than in the office — all books, all music, all songs. . . .

It is a matter of striving, pursuing the goal, running after it, and eventually catching it to a certain degree and bringing it into realization.

Question: If I were to give my children these visualizations, which one should I start with?

Answer: If it is a child I would ask, "Do you see this rose?" "Yes." "Is it beautiful? Look at it very nicely." He looks and says, "It is red, but there are yellow hues and petals like this and leaves are like that. Oh, Mommy, how beautiful is the rose." Now when you take the reality approach, you say, "Can you close your eyes? See if you can see a rose with closed eyes." You do not say visualization. He looks and looks and says, "No Mommy, I cannot see anything." "All right. Do it again." Another day do it again, again. Eventually, if the child in the past worked, he will say, "I see the rose perfectly there." Then you can increase, using different flowers, different trees. Then you create dances, symphonies, this or that. It is a whole curriculum.

For example, if I take this whole Aquarian Educational Group and put it only in the visualization track, we have fifty years of specialized work to do. We gave you a general background, great literature. We gave you supreme ideas on how to live, how to relate, but we did not start yet this kind of job. You can develop by yourself because the books are there.

Question: The second time you did the visualization, I saw everything in three dimensions. The box was not just a square; it was a box. The first time I saw just the two dimensional square, triangle, and circle, but the second time everything turned spherical, like the triangle was a pyramid, and the circle was a whole sphere. Then I was worried about the cross. Would it be only one cross or four, like the four sides of the box. At that time I got confused because I was hot inside, like hot flashes from doing something wrong, and then later you said about the sphere and I cooled down a bit. Was it okay?

Answer: When these kinds of psychological turmoil happen within you, you are going to say, "Cool down," and start from the beginning. Start always from the beginning. Then develop it. Then again it returns. Start from the beginning. Fifty times, two hundred times start from the beginning. Then things will start to be clearer, clearer, clearer. It is not the object that is not clear. It is your mind. So, as the mind exercises, it learns how to do things.

Question: I could not get the red square because I was the red square. If you cannot visualize the red square, should you go on to visualize the white cross and the triangle and the circle?

Answer: You can do it but eventually you are going to go to the beginning again. Let me find the square and nail it on the wall and see four sides. Then I break it and bring it down and make the square big and enter into it and feel the walls and get out and nail the walls together to make the square, until I make it real. Unreality will disappear. You will play games to make this square really impressed in your mind. I put apples in it and then throw the apples out and close the door. Then I make doors and windows until I create something that, through association, the square stays in my mind. Then I take a cross and nail it. Then the cross shifts like this. Okay, I will do it slowly, slowly, until my mind, do not forget this, through exercise gains control over the mental plane. When the control is there, the result immediately is there. This is fantastic. I cannot explain to you how valuable is this lesson.

Question: What is the advantage of doing these exercises for gaining emotional control?

Answer: You must not try to control emotions with these symbols. Your emotional body is part of humanity's astral body in which millions of currents exist. This will take us until morning. Do not approach emotions. When you are visualizing, keep it in the mental plane.

Question: There was an exercise you gave us a long time ago about walking a tightrope between two mountains. You talked about coordinating the mind and the emotions.

Answer: That is totally different. If I give a physical exercise, for example, I say to walk on this line from mountain top to mountain top, that is physical. Then I do emotional, then I do mental. These symbols are not just for control of the bodies. You are controlling your fear, your anxiety, not the body. When you read the books you will understand very clearly because I tried to make things clear as much as possible.

Question: I could see the square and cross and triangle, but then it would fluctuate slightly, but when I saw the sphere, I could control it.

Answer: It is very possible and probable until by experience you gain control over the mental substance. It will take time. You never blame yourself that you did not learn anything. I think all of you learned a very valuable lesson.

I wish that there were thousands of people here joining in our labor. My last suggestion is this: Form little groups at your home who meet once a week and do these exercises.

Summary — *Lesson Four, part one*

1. Close your eyes.
2. See a square box. Open it and enter into it. Close the lid. Feel the walls. Count the walls and feel them.
3. Get out of the box and look at it. Make it bigger and bigger. Then make it smaller, until it is one inch.
4. Make the box yellow. All yellow.
5. Make it yellow on one side and white on the other. Take it in your hand and examine it. Make it all red.
6. Nail it on the wall.
7. Nail a white cross on it.
8. Put a blue triangle around the box.
9. Work very slowly and imagine or visualize this combination: red square box, white cross, blue triangle. Work until it is clear.
10. Put a circle around the whole group. Make it a violet, fiery circle.

11. Push the square far away. Push the triangle far away. See how they look in the frame of the circle.
12. Rest for five minutes.

— Lesson Four, part two

1. Again see the red box on the wall. Nail the white cross on it. Put a blue triangle around it. Put a violet circle around it. Build each part slowly and deliberately. Keep your eyebrows, neck, and teeth relaxed.
2. Push the square away from you, and then bring it forward. Repeat.
3. Go and touch the red box. Feel it. See it. Nail on it a white cross. See how your fingers are moving. Add the triangle and circle, being conscious how you are adding them. The circle is a transparent sphere.
4. When you are done, open your eyes and rub your forehead and eyebrows.

Note: Do this exercise in the right sequence, as given.

About the Author

This booklet is a transcription of a series of classes given by Torkom Saraydarian in 1996.

The author's books have been used all over the world as sources of guidance and inspiration for those seeking to live a life based on the teachings of the Ageless Wisdom. Some of the books have been translated into other languages, including Armenian, German, Dutch, Danish, Portuguese, Spanish, Italian, Greek, Yugoslavian, and Swedish.

Torkom Saraydarian's entire life was a zealous effort to help people live healthy, joyous, and successful lives. He spread this message of love and true vision tirelessly throughout his life. From early boyhood the author learned first-hand from teachers of the Ageless Wisdom. He studied widely in the world's religions and philosophies. In addition, he was an accomplished pianist, violinist, and cellist, and played many other instruments as well. His books, lectures, seminars, and music have inspired and continue to offer a true insight into the beauty of the Ageless Wisdom.

Torkom Saraydarian (1915-1997) has left a huge legacy for all those who seek to strive and continuously labor to improve themselves.

Index

Other Books by Torkom Saraydarian

The Ageless Wisdom
The Bhagavad Gita
Battling Dark Forces
Breakthrough to Higher Psychism
Buddha Sutra — A Dialogue with the Glorious One
Challenge for Discipleship
Christ, The Avatar of Sacrificial Love
A Commentary on Psychic Energy
Cosmic Shocks
Cosmos in Man
The Creative Fire
Dynamics of Success
The Flame of Beauty, Culture, Love, Joy
The Flame of the Heart
From My Heart - Vol. I (Poetry)
Hiawatha and the Great Peace
The Hidden Glory of the Inner Man
I Was
Joy and Healing
Leadership Vol. I
Leadership Vol. II
Leadership Vol. III
Legend of Shamballa
The Mystery of Self-Image
The Mysteries of Willpower
New Dimensions in Healing
Olympus World Report . . .The Year 3000
One Hundred Names of God
Other Worlds
The Psyche and Psychism (Two Volume Set)
The Psychology of Cooperation and Group Consciousness

The Purpose of Life
The Science of Becoming Oneself
The Science of Meditation
The Sense of Responsibility in Society
Sex, Family, and the Woman in Society
The Solar Angel
Spiritual Regeneration
The Subconscious Mind and the Chalice
Symphony of the Zodiac
Talks on Agni
Thought and the Glory of Thinking
Triangles of Fire
Unusual Court
Woman, Torch of the Future
The Year 2000 & After

Booklets

A Daily Discipline of Worship
Cornerstones of Health
Daily Spiritual Striving
Discipleship in Action
Duties of Grandparents
Earthquakes and Disasters, What the Ageless Wisdom Tells Us
Fiery Carriage and Drugs
Five Great Mantrams of the New Age
Hierarchy and the Plan
How to Find Your Level of Meditation
Inner Blooming
Irritation — The Destructive Fire
Mental Exercises
Nachiketas
New Beginnings
Practical Spirituality
Questioning Traveler and Karma
Saint Sergius
Spring of Prosperity
Synthesis

Booklets (Excerpts and Compilations)

Angels and Devas
Building Family Unity
Courage
First Steps Toward Freedom
Responsibility
Responsibility and Business
Responsibilities of Fathers
Responsibilities of Mothers
Prayers, Mantrams & Invocations
The Psychology of Cooperation
Success
The Chalice in Agni Yoga Literature
Torchbearers
What to Look for in the Heart of Your Partner

Music (Composed and Performed by Torkom Saraydarian)

A Touch of Heart (CD) Piano
Dance of the Zodiac (Cassette) Solo Piano
Far Horizons (Cassette) Solo Piano
Fire Blossom (Cassette) Solo Piano
Infinity (Cassette) Solo Piano
Lao Tse (Cassette) Solo Piano
Light Years Ahead (Cassette) Solo Piano
Lily in Tibet (Cassette) Solo Piano
Misty Mountains (Cassette) Solo Piano
Piano Compositions (Cassette)
Rainbow (Cassette) Solo Piano & Cello
Spirit of My Heart (Cassette) Voice & Multi-instrument
Sun Rhythms (Cassette) Oud, Cello, Drum
Tears of My Joy (Cassette) Solo Piano

• • •

Go In Beauty (Cassette) - 19 Mantrams & Songs Sung by AEG Choir

Videos

The Seven Rays Interpreted
(Video interview with Torkom Saraydarian regarding *The Great Invocation* and the Seven Rays)

Video Lecture Tapes by Torkom Saraydarian
(Audio lecture tapes also available)

Ordering Information

Write to the publisher for additional information regarding:

- Free catalog of author's books and music tapes
- Audio lecture tapes and videos; complete list available
- Placement on mailing list
- New releases and recent information
- A free copy of our newsletter *Outreach*

Additional copies of -

The Art of Visualization
U.S. $6.00
Postage within U.S.A. – $3.00
Plus applicable state sales tax
International postage: contact us for rates
(Specify air or surface mail)

T.S.G. Publishing Foundation, Inc.
P. O. Box 7068
Cave Creek, AZ 85327-7068
United States of America
TEL: (602) 502-1909
FAX: (602) 502-0713

T.S.G. Publishing Foundation, Inc. is a non-profit, tax-exempt organization.

Our purpose is to be a pathway for self-transformation. We offer books, audio and video tapes, classes and seminars, and home study courses based on the core values and higher principles of the Ageless Wisdom.

From our founding in 1987, we have been devoted to publishing, distributing, and teaching the works of Torkom Saraydarian. Torkom has left us many books that remain to be released. We will continue our efforts to make them available to all of you.

These books have been published by the generous donations of the students of the Ageless Wisdom from all over the world.

Your tax deductible contributions will help us continue publishing and growing.

We are deeply grateful for your continued love and support.

The Art of Visualization

Simply Presented

These symbols — square, cross, triangle, circle — eventually turn into transmitters. Each symbol is an extension of the Intuitional Plane. That is why studying and meditating about the symbols and visualizing the symbols make an access to the Intuitional Plane. . . .Then in the Intuitional Plane, an intuitional form is formed. It radiates to different layers, different people, different centers, and it becomes a radio station bringing you ideas, beautiful ideas.

Eventually the destination of disciples is not worship but entering into the subjective world, the world of energies, forces, and current . . .

Torkom Saraydarian

U.S. $6.00